EARTH'S
HISTORY
THROUGH
ROCKS

LAVA AND MAGMA

HOW
THE HAWAIIAN ISLANDS
FORMED

JEREMY MORLOCK

PowerKiDS
press.

New York

Published in 2020 by The Rosen Publishing Group, Inc.
29 East 21st Street, New York, NY 10010

First Edition

Editor: Sarah Machajewski
Book Design: Tanya Dellaccio

Photo Credits: Cover Sky Noir Photography by Bill Dickinson/Moment/Getty Images; p. 5 Stocktrek Images/Getty Images; p. 7 (top) www.sandatlas.org/Shutterstock.com; pp. 7 (bottom), 22, 23 Courtesy of the United States Geology Survey; p. 9 Lisa Hoang/Shutterstock.com; p. 11 (top) Ron Bull/Toronto Star/Getty Images; p. 11 (bottom) QAI Publishing/Universal Images Group/Getty Images; p. 13 (top) Maridav/Shutterstock.com; pp. 13 (bottom), 19 Mario Tama/Getty Images News/Getty Images; p. 15 https://upload.wikimedia.org/wikipedia/commons/0/0f/Mauna_Kea_from_Mauna_Loa_Observatory%2C_Hawaii_-_20100913.jpg; p. 17 (top) George Rose/Getty Images News/Getty Images; pp. 17 (bottom), 21 Anadolu Agency/Getty Images; p. 18 VW Pics/Universal Images Group/Getty Images; p. 25 Andriy Prokopenko/Moment/Getty Images; p. 27 (top) Miguel Pereira/Cover/Getty Images; p. 27 (bottom) John Seaton Callahan/Moment/Getty Images; p. 29 Thinkstock/Stockbyte/Getty Images; p. 30 Felix Nendzig/Shutterstock.com.

Library of Congress Cataloging-in-Publication Data

Names: Morlock, Jeremy (Jeremy P.), author.
Title: Lava and magma : how the Hawaiian Islands formed / Jeremy Morlock.
Description: New York : PowerKids Press, [2020] | Series: Earth's history
  through rocks | Includes index.
Identifiers: LCCN 2018058708| ISBN 9781725301481 (pbk.) | ISBN 9781725301504
  (library bound) | ISBN 9781725301498 (6 pack)
Subjects: LCSH: Geology–Hawaii–Juvenile literature. |
  Volcanoes–Hawaii–Juvenile literature. | Volcanism–Hawaii–Juvenile
  literature. | Hawaii–Juvenile literature.
Classification: LCC QE349.H3 M67 2020 | DDC 559.69–dc23
LC record available at https://lccn.loc.gov/2018058708

Manufactured in the United States of America

CPSIA Compliance Information: Batch #CSPK19. For Further Information contact Rosen Publishing, New York, New York at 1-800-237-9932.

CONTENTS

THE HAWAIIAN ISLANDS

The state of Hawaii is composed of 137 islands in the Pacific Ocean, thousands of miles away from the mainland United States. Some of the islands are tiny, but some are much larger. People live on the seven biggest islands. The state's largest island, which itself is named Hawaii, is also called the Big Island. It's more than 4,000 square miles (10,360 sq. km).

What made the islands? Why are they so far away from other land? These are questions people have wondered since the first **Polynesian** settlers came to live in Hawaii more than 1,000 years ago. The huge and powerful forces that created the Hawaiian Islands left behind clues in the rocks found there. These forces are still making their mark, and the changes happening today tell us a lot about the past.

AN ARCHIPELAGO AT SEA

The Hawaiian Islands are an **archipelago**. The Hawaiian archipelago includes reefs and atolls. Reefs are ridges near the surface of the water. They can be made of rocks or sand. Reefs can also be made of corals, which are tiny animals that live underwater, and the layers of minerals they **excrete**. An atoll is a ring-shaped coral island.

KAUAI

NIIHAU

OAHU

MOLOKAI

MAUI

LANAI

KAHOOLAWE

HAWAII

The larger islands of Niihau, Kauai, Oahu, Molokai, Lanai, Kahoolawe, Maui, and Hawaii can be seen in this picture taken by a **satellite**. No one lives on Kahoolawe, the smallest of the eight.

STUDYING HAWAII'S PAST AND PRESENT

From the shape of its mountains to the feel of its dirt, every aspect of Hawaii's geological features gives us clues about its past. Geologists are scientists who study the processes that shape Earth. Some of these processes happen quickly, while others take a long time.

Hawaii's islands began as volcanoes that erupted at the bottom of the ocean. A volcano is an opening in Earth's crust from which molten rock, gas, and other material escape from inside the planet. This is called an eruption.

The volcanoes that created the Hawaiian Islands began erupting millions of years ago. The lava cooled and hardened into rock, and it built up more layers with each new eruption. Eventually, the islands began rising above the water's surface.

A geologist measures the temperature of a crack in the ground caused by a volcano. She learned it was 200°F (93°C). ▶

READING THE ROCKS

MOLTEN ROCK IS CALLED MAGMA WHEN IT'S INSIDE THE EARTH. WHEN IT FLOWS ONTO EARTH'S SURFACE, IT'S CALLED LAVA. COOLED AND HARDENED LAVA FORMS IGNEOUS ROCK.

A HOT SPOT UNDER THE OCEAN

The theory of plate tectonics explains that the ground beneath our feet is constantly moving. This explains why there are seven continents on Earth and how volcanic islands such as the Hawaiian Islands formed. According to this theory, Earth's **lithosphere** is made of large plates. These huge pieces of solid rock slowly float on top of the lower mantle, which is made of soft, **fluid** rock.

Most volcanoes form in places where tectonic plates are pushing against or pulling away from each other. However, Hawaii is on the Pacific plate in a location far from its edges. Scientists needed a new theory to explain how those islands formed. Now they believe that a hot spot under the ocean created the volcanoes.

Diamond Head crater on the island of Oahu was made by a volcanic eruption about 300,000 years ago. The materials thrown out of the volcano settled together and formed a kind of rock called tuff. ▶

A HOTBED OF ACTIVITY

Hot spots form when a tectonic plate moves over a very hot part of Earth's lower mantle. Magma rises and, with extreme levels of heat and pressure, pushes through the solid crust. The very hot part stays in a fixed location, while the plate above moves away from it. This is how chains of islands form. They're sometimes called hot spot tracks.

A CHAIN OF VOLCANOES

The chain of islands that is Hawaii was likely created by a hot spot under the Pacific plate. As the plate moved, the first islands stopped growing and new ones formed from new volcanic eruptions. For many years, scientists thought the hot spot stayed in place while the plate moved. Now, some think the hot spot moves too.

The chain of Hawaiian islands also includes underwater mountains called seamounts. Geologists call this trail of volcanoes the Hawaiian-Emperor seamount chain. The newest mountains and islands are closest to the volcanoes that are still active. The youngest seamount in the Hawaiian chain is called Loihi. If it continues to grow, it will eventually become the next island in the chain.

A chain of volcanoes is created as a tectonic plate moves over a hot spot. ▶

J. TUZO WILSON

The Canadian geophysicist J. Tuzo Wilson came up with the hot spot theory. He wrote a paper in 1963 to tell other scientists about it. As a model, Wilson used paper as the tectonic plate and a candle as the hot spot. He'd move the paper above the candle. The heat would turn the paper brown along a path. This was like the chain of volcanoes over the hot spot.

MAGMA AND LAVA

Beneath volcanoes, the **intense** heat and pressure are strong enough to melt surrounding rock. Gases can become trapped inside the melted material. Magma is less **dense** than solid rock, and it rises through openings in Earth's layers. When it comes to Earth's surface, lava can act differently than it did when it was magma.

The differences can depend on the types of rocks and minerals that melted together underground. They can also depend on what's happening below the ground. Sometimes gas will leak out, but other times it will form bubbles within the magma. This is why some volcanoes have violent, fiery eruptions, while others have lava slowly seep from them. With Hawaiian volcanoes, lava usually emerges slowly.

TYPES OF ERUPTIONS

When liquid lava pours out of a vent, it's called an effusive eruption. In this type of eruption, lava can shoot up like a fountain or flow like a river. When bubbles of gas inside magma make it burst and pop, it is called an explosive eruption. In this type of eruption, solid rock and lava are thrown through the air. Sometimes eruptions push out just gas and not lava.

Lava flowing from the Kilauea volcano on Hawaii's Big Island moves downhill into the ocean.

13

VOLCANO FORMATION

Volcanoes have different shapes based on how lava flows from them. Some are steep and cone shaped. Others are wide with gently sloped sides. These are called shield volcanoes. Geologists thought these volcanoes looked like shields lying on the ground.

Hawaii has huge shield volcanoes. Slow-flowing lava builds up in layers to make the shield shape. As the lava flows, cools, and hardens many, many times, the volcano spreads out and gets wider. These volcanoes are tallest at the vent, near where the lava exits.

There are shield volcanoes in Idaho, Arizona, Washington, Oregon, and California. There are also shield volcanoes in the Galápagos Islands, Iceland, and Africa.

READING THE ROCKS

SCIENTISTS USE REMOTE-CONTROLLED SEACRAFT TO GATHER EVIDENCE ABOUT UNDERWATER VOLCANIC ERUPTIONS. THE CRAFT'S **SONAR** RECORDS MEASUREMENTS OF UNDERWATER MASSES AND OBJECTS, SUCH AS HILLS OF LAVA ON THE SEAFLOOR.

This photograph of the Mauna Kea volcano shows its shield shape, formed by many lava flows.

ACTIVE, DORMANT, AND EXTINCT

There are three **categories** of volcanoes: active, dormant, and extinct. These categories are based on what the volcanoes are expected to do. Active volcanoes have erupted recently or are showing signs of activity, such as gas coming from the vent. Dormant volcanoes haven't erupted in a long time, but they may in the future. They're in a quiet time between periods of activity. Extinct volcanoes were active long ago, but they're not expected to erupt again.

The time between volcanic eruptions can be tens of thousands of years. This means it can be difficult to tell if a volcano is actually extinct or if it's dormant. The Hawaiian archipelago has volcanoes in each category. The Kilauea volcano on the island of Hawaii has been active for more than 35 years.

READING THE ROCKS

THE BIG ISLAND HAS FIVE VOLCANOES: KOHALA, MAUNA KEA, HUALALAI, MAUNA LOA, AND KILAUEA. KOHALA IS THE OLDEST. GEOLOGISTS HAVE STUDIED THE LAYERS OF ROCK FROM PAST ERUPTIONS. THEY THINK KOHALA LAST ERUPTED 60,000 YEARS AGO.

In the spring and summer of 2018, lava flowed from parts of the Kilauea volcano and earthquakes shook the area.

POLYNESIAN TRADITIONS

Polynesian peoples settled islands in the Pacific Ocean and were the first to live in Hawaii. Polynesian traditional stories tell of the creation of the Hawaiian Islands. One story says that the **demigod** Maui was fishing with his brothers and using a fishhook that had special powers. When the brothers pulled the fishing line, the hook brought up land from beneath the ocean. This land is now the Hawaiian Islands.

Other stories tell of Pele, a goddess who controls volcanoes and fire. Her power creates and destroys, and Pele shapes the land. The stories say that volcano craters on different islands are the places she built fire pits. Pele has an important place in Hawaiian culture. Some Hawaiians continue to honor Pele today.

People left offerings to Pele in front of lava from Kilauea that flowed through the Leilani Estates neighborhood in May 2018.

DANGER AND DESTRUCTION

Magma is extremely hot. The magma inside Kilauea can reach 2,120°F (1,160°C). In addition to the very hot temperatures, volcanoes pose other dangers. New cracks in the ground, called fissures, can open up because of underground pressure. During eruptions, lava and dangerous gases come through vents. Water touching lava creates hot steam.

Pieces of rock thrown into the air during an eruption are called tephra. Tephra includes volcanic ash. Larger rocks may be dangerous as they fall from the air or move downhill. In 2018, part of the summit, or top, of Kilauea collapsed. In one spot, a fountain of lava shot 250 feet (76.2 m) into the air. Lava poured from fissures and destroyed hundreds of homes. Thousands of people had to evacuate to stay safe from lava, fire, ash, and gas.

READING THE ROCKS

THE TYPE OF ERUPTIONS THAT HAPPENED AT KILAUEA IN 2018 ALSO HAPPENED THERE MILLIONS OF YEARS AGO. GEOLOGISTS KNOW ABOUT THIS DANGEROUS PAST BECAUSE OF CLUES IN THE ROCK LAYERS AND SHAPES FOUND NEARBY.

This photo from May 2018 shows lava destroying homes and buildings on the island of Hawaii.

VOLCANIC CREATIONS

An eruption doesn't just destroy. It can create new things too. Flowing lava adds new surface rock to an island, creating more places for animals, plants, and sometimes people to live. When lava flies through the air, the minerals inside can turn into pieces of glass called Pele's hair. This is when tiny pieces of hot volcanic glass are stretched long and thin as they fall. The air carries them away and they can pile up when they land.

Pele's tears are bits of black volcanic glass that cool into a **sphere** or teardrop shape. Sometimes they're attached to one end of a piece of Pele's hair. Lava trees form when hot lava covers a tree and burns it away. The lava cools in the shape of the tree that was there.

PELE'S HAIR

Flowing and splashing lava cools into lava trees where living trees once stood.

TIME AND TIDES

The Hawaiian Islands formed thousands of years ago, but other forces are shaping them today. The rocks and tephra that built the islands have been worn down and moved around through a process called weathering.

Weathering happens when forces such as wind and rain beat against the rocks and loosen particles. Weathering can also include chemical changes. Erosion happens when water or wind wear away rock and carry particles away. Usually, these forces carry rock pieces to lower ground and into the ocean. Rain gathers into streams and rivers that cut a path through the land. At the edges of the Hawaiian Islands, ocean waves and tides mean that the water is always crashing against the land. These forces created valleys, cliffs, shores, and other landforms around Hawaii.

Waves crash against rocks on the edge of the island of Kauai at Nāpali Coast State Park.

FERTILE SOIL

As lava and ash break down, they mix with other materials, such as dead plants and rainwater. Together, this mixture becomes soil in which new plants take root.

Hawaiian soil can be very **fertile** because of chemicals, such as calcium and potassium, that came from volcanoes. They provide important nutrients for plants. Fertile soil also contains the right amount of water to keep plants healthy.

Hawaii has many soil types. Soil forms differently high up a mountain than it does on low land near the coast. Many plants growing in Hawaii aren't found anywhere else in the world. It takes many years for fertile soil to form. However, some plants can start to grow over a lava flow in less than a year.

FARMING IN HAWAII

Hawaii's fertile soil also helps people grow healthy plants. The Polynesian people first grew and ate plants such as sweet potatoes, taro, and bananas. Later, other people brought fruits such as oranges and pineapples to Hawaii and planted these crops. For many years, sugar and pineapple were major crops on the islands. They were grown in Hawaii and often sold far away. Macadamia nuts and coffee also grow well in volcanic soil.

Rain and rich soil help plants grow in the Hanalei Valley of the island of Kauai.

A CHANGING COASTLINE

Many people travel to Hawaii to marvel at its white, pink, and black sand beaches. This sand is made of many things, including tiny pieces of coral and shell from reefs near the islands. Broken-down volcanic rock also becomes sand. The movement of water leaves sand along the edges of the islands.

Beaches change when water leaves more sand or washes it away. In recent years, more sand has been washed away than has been set down. Scientists measure changes in the weather and the water. They've compared those to measurements from past years. They learned that the level of the ocean is rising. Bigger storms also are happening more often. This speeds up erosion, and sand washes away faster.

BELOW THE WAVES

In October 2018, Hurricane Walaka hit the French Frigate Shoals, a Hawaiian atoll made up of a reef and small islands. When the hurricane ended, one of the islands had eroded so much that it was completely underwater. No people had lived there, but it had been an important place for seals, turtles, and birds to rest and raise their young.

The volcanic cone Puʻu Olai rises above sandy beaches at Makena State Park on the island of Maui.

CHANGES CONTINUE

The land around us is changing all the time. Some changes are slow, such as the weathering of rock. It can take years, or hundreds of years, for us to notice these changes. Some changes are fast, like the eruption of lava. Eruptions can be so quick and huge that they can be dangerous.

Volcanoes built up the Hawaiian Islands. Wind and water helped shape them. Weathering and erosion wear down high mountains. Some of the islands made by older volcanoes are now underwater. At the same time, the young Loihi volcano is growing underwater. The Kilauea volcano has added new land to the Big Island. These forces of creation and destruction shaped Hawaii's past and will shape its future.

GLOSSARY

archipelago: A group or chain of islands close together in a body of water.

category: Class or group.

demigod: Someone with more power than a human but less than a god.

dense: Packed very closely together.

excrete: In a living organism, to separate and give off as waste.

fertile: Capable of producing healthy and strong plants.

fluid: Flowing freely.

intense: Existing to an extreme degree.

lithosphere: Earth's crust and upper mantle.

Polynesian: Of Polynesia, islands of the central and southern Pacific Ocean.

satellite: A machine that travels around Earth, a moon, or another planet in order to collect information about it.

sonar: A machine that uses sound waves to find things in a body of water.

sphere: A three-dimensional object shaped like a ball.

INDEX

WEBSITES

Due to the changing nature of Internet links, PowerKids Press has developed an online list of websites related to the subject of this book. This site is updated regularly. Please use this link to access the list: www.powerkidslinks.com/EHTR/islands